Bread (

MW01122832

Contents

written by Diana Freeman

1

To make your own bread you will need:
White flour   Whole wheat flour
Dry yeast   Honey
Milk   Water   Salt

First you need to warm a large bowl. Then put in one tablespoon of yeast.

3

Add one tablespoon of honey.
Then add one large cup of warm
milk and water mixed together.
Leave this mixture in a warm
place for ten minutes.

Warm two bread tins and wipe them inside with oil.
(This is so that the bread won't stick to the tins when it is baked.)

After ten minutes, the mixture will be fizzy with bubbles.
Mix in one large teaspoon of salt.
Then mix in two cups of white flour and two cups of whole wheat flour.

Stir in another large cup
of warm milk and water.
The mixture will be sticky
and sloppy.
This is called dough.

Put the dough into two bread tins
and cover it with a clean cloth.
Leave it to rise in a warm place
for about 30 minutes.
Turn on the oven to heat up to
350 degrees F or 180 degrees C.

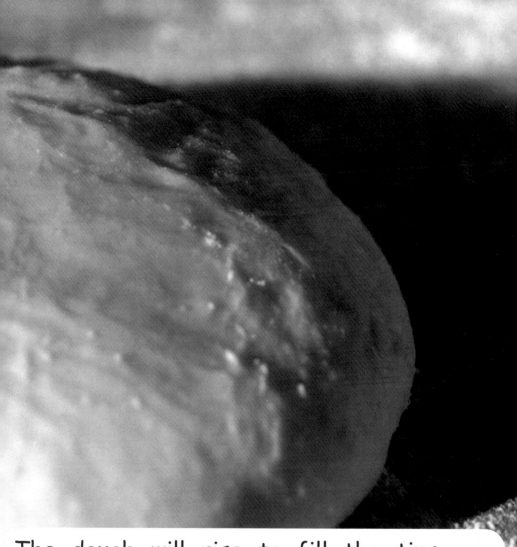

The dough will rise to fill the tins.
It will be twice as big as it was before!
Put the tins into the hot oven.
Leave the bread to bake for about
40 minutes.

Take out your homemade bread.
Let it cool for ten minutes before
you cut it.

Put some homemade butter on the warm bread and taste it. It will be delicious!

This is one way you can make butter.
Pour one cup of cream into a jar.
Then add half a teaspoon of salt.
Put the lid on tightly, and begin to
shake the jar.

You can pass the jar around a group of friends, so that everyone has a turn. The cream will soon begin to get lumpy. You will see lumps of yellow butter and some buttermilk.

After shaking the jar for about 15 minutes, you will have one large lump. Open the jar, and take out your homemade butter.

It's ready to put on your homemade bread!
How delicious!